Maybe,

It's Just Me…

by Pastor Nancy Advincola

DORRANCE
PUBLISHING CO
EST. 1920
PITTSBURGH, PENNSYLVANIA 15238

Dorrance Publishing Co
585 Alpha Drive
Suite 103
Pittsburgh, PA 15238
Visit our website at www.dorrancebookstore.com

ISBN: 978-1-6442-6276-4
eISBN: 978-1-6442-6412-6

1 Thessalonians 5:11 (ESV)
Therefore encourage one another and build one another up, just as you are doing.

Encouragement is awesome. It (can) change the course of another person's day, week, or life.
~ Chuck Swindoll

TABLE OF CONTENTS

My Expression of Gratitude

To my Lord and Savior, the Alpha and Omega, Jesus, the Son of God, the only one who saved, transformed and impacted my life in such a way, all I want to do all day, is praise His Holy name. (hallelujah). Without any doubt, Christ has brought purpose, meaning and an abundance of forgiveness and love into my life (alleluia).

To the man of my dreams, the one who Christ used to teach me how to laugh, love and happily enjoy this adventure we call life. My darling husband of 30 genuinely blessed years, three months and 25 days, Pastor Carlos Ramon Advincola, Sr. aka my Gem, Dominican Danish and so many other sweet names.

To the fruit of our endless love, the gifts from above and the bundles of joy after we happily said "I Do" to each other. By the grace of God, I'm referring to the four Diamond and daring sons, which the Lord blessed us with:

- Carlos Ramon Advincola, Jr.
- Josue' Agustin Advincola
- Esteban Gabriel Advincola, and
- Elias Jacob Advincola

To the people who encouraged me during my entire life, and they're also the key to who I am today...my beloved parents, who are (both) home with the Lord. My Mommy Judy LaGuerre, who sat next to me (all night) in the kitchen when I had lots of homework and helped me study for my tests, too. During that time, that my Momi kept me company, she always had a smile on her face and prayed with me when I couldn't sleep, she was awesome and sweet that way. Now, let's talk about my outspoken Papi Pablo Curet Sr., a strong-minded man, teddy bear, who always felt the need to speak, instruct, guide and fill my siblings and me with all kinds of sweet goodies, in my eyes, he was my Mr. Softy.

I've also been blessed to have two loving, respectful and caring in-laws. My mother-in-law, Manuela (Madre) Valdez, was a strong-minded and caring individual. No one, I mean "no one" went to bed hungry, while she was alive… accompanied by, my dear and loving father-in-law, Emilio (Chori) Amador, he was a soft-spoken man, hardworking and an extremely strict parental figure. Before they went home with the Lord, I clearly understood why my husband is the sweetest individual; I've ever met. As for my in-laws, they were terrific parents, and they left me with the kindest man on this planet, my husband.

With a smile on my face and childhood memories (of laughter) flowing around in my mind, I'd like to thank my little brother, Pablo Curet Jr. aka Tono, for continually reminding me that the letters I used to write him were so long that it took him hours to read. You were such a supportive force (in such an amusing way), and that's why I'm so grateful to say, that you're a lovely contribution to my writing career.

Before I bring this appreciation page to an end, I'd like to thank Dorrance Publishing for welcoming my book into the community of upcoming and already established authors; I'm honored to be among all of you.

And last, but certainly not least, I want to thank every one of you, for taking the time to purchase and read my book.

I'd like to share with all of you my favorite Bible verse and quote:

Proverbs 10:22 (NLT)
The blessings of the LORD makes a person rich, and He adds no sorrow with it.

"God has written His divine guidelines for your life right in the Bible."
~ Elizabeth George

Preface

The preamble of this book came into existence when I finally allowed my heart to have full reign over what I was writing. It was an ongoing process for me; because I was always debating with myself about what events should or shouldn't be in this book. After I finally wrapped my arms around those memories orchestrated by Christ, everything "finally" fell into place (thank You, Jesus).

I firmly believe that If I'd gone "Cold Turkey" on the over-analyzing of everything, I wouldn't encounter so much tossing and turning during the night. Oh well, lesson learned and primarily based upon this bible verses.

Proverbs 3:5-6 (GNT)

5. Trust in the Lord with all your heart. Never rely on what you think you know.
6. Remember the Lord in everything you do, and He will show you the right way.

Ask for what you want but always be willing to take what God gives. It may prove better than what you ask for.

~ Norman Vincent Peale

Care to continue this journey with me? If so, before you read any further, here are some suggestions that's if you truly desire to embrace what Jesus Christ has nested in my mind, heart, and life!

All you need to do is prepare a cup of coffee, tea or perhaps, some sweet hot cocoa (whatever tickles your fancy) and then find a comfy spot in your apartment, house or car and oh yes, don't forget to reflect on this.

Romans 12:12 (HCSB)

Do not be conformed to this age, but be transformed by the renewing of your mind, so that you may discern what the good, pleasing, and perfect will of God are.

> Make sure you're committed to Jesus Christ and seek to follow Him every day. Don't be swayed by the false values and goals of this World, but put Christ and His will first in everything you do.
> ~ Billy Graham

Ladies and Gentlemen, feel free to read on with me.

Introduction

Everyone has a reason for what they feel, say or do, and this is my motive for writing this book.

Matthew 6:21 (NLT)
Wherever your treasure is, there the desires of your heart will also be.

> "Life is not about receiving at all times; it is a combination of being thankful for what you have as blessings and sharing those blessings with others who need a little fraction of what you have."
> ~ Catherine Pulsifer

Yes and by all means, I want to share with the world my triumphs and unexpected sorrows, how I felt once they arrived and what trials and tribulations accompanied them. Because in life you can't have one without the other. Painful moments will eventually lead to life lessons (speaking from experience). That's why I'm confident that some or all of you must have experienced something similar or perhaps entirely different of what I'm writing.

On the other hand, I know (deep in my heart) that whatever you and I have been through, it's because Jesus Christ wants to birth something positive out of it. This way you and I can delight in what God has blessed us with and impact all those around us, too. Moreover, the Lord wanted you and I to take this opportunity to share helpful advice with a sibling, friend, co-worker or an acquaintance also. Why don't you try this Biblical advice on for size?

Proverbs 9:9 (NOG)

Advise a wise person, and he will become even more knowledgeable. Teach a righteous person, and he will learn more.

> "The goodness you receive from God is a treasure for you to share with others."
>
> ~ Elizabeth George

Chapter One ~ Finally

Most or all of you are probably wondering why I chose to title this first chapter "Finally." Well, allow me to explain? When I was putting all my thoughts on paper, I knew the internet is faster; however, I'm an Old School kind of Gal, that still believes in writing down all my ideas on paper. Then I proceeded to subtract what isn't needed, arrange everything according to the events and "Finally" I typed and saved everything until the next day when I proofread it all over again. Maybe, that's just me, but that's how I decided to call this first chapter "Finally."

Perchance, most of you lovely readers might be curious on why I chose to write this book at such a slow pace, instead of typing at the speed of a train (for today's society). My dear friends, here's my reply to why I chose to write first and then type later.

> Colossians 3:23 (ISV)
> Whatever you do, work at it wholeheartedly as though you were doing it for the Lord and not merely for people.

> We should live our lives as if Christ is coming this afternoon.
> ~ Jimmy Carter

Every word I typed was with the sole purpose that this book ministers to the lives of those who read this book and not to obtain fame. But, you'll see what I mean while you accompany me on this journey I call "life." As a special treat, I'm also sharing a few pep talks; so that they can make a way to a more effective learning experience. Keep in mind, that all of the above information was done for the Lord's glory and the delight of each of you, too.

To my morning, afternoon and night time readers, do you know that during the most agonizing moments of my life and after a good cry (that's right), a profound cry that reaches the King of Kings in His throne, then I'd study the word with more intensity, and this is what I learned.

2 Corinthians 4:8-9 (NIV)

8. We are pressed on every side, but we still have room to move. We are often in much trouble, but we never give up.
9. People made it hard for us, but we are not left alone. We are knocked down, but we are not destroyed.

> "Don't ever discount the wonder of your tears. They can be healing waters and a stream of joy. Sometimes they are the best words the heart can speak."
> ~ William Paul Young

During the typing and revising of each word and sentence, I hope that all of you receive comfort and confidence, especially during those painful moments of your life. Everybody, why don't you make believe your sitting in my living room (right next to me), and delighting in a cup of tea with a plate of crackers and cheese (that's how I savor my reading time). I'm sharing various details with all of you because the steps I took before, during and after I pick up a book symbolize that I don't just want to rush through each page as if it was a flyer of the items sold in the neighborhood supermarket or something of little interest. In my opinion, books are sources of learning something new, as well as uncovering what is going on in the author's mind and heart when he or she wrote their book.

Maybe, It's Just Me, but my goal is to grasp the plot and relate to the characters' feelings and "Finally" contemplate whether or not I agree or not with the ending. Nonetheless, I know in my heart that whatever I read, there's always going to be a vital lesson for me to learn and share with those in need, too. Is any of this hitting home with someone? If it is, then the Glory is always for the Creator of Heaven and earth. You know what, it is time for me to study the word some more and this is why.

2 Timothy 3:16 (NCV)
All Scripture is inspired by God and is useful for teaching, for showing people what is wrong in their lives, by correcting faults, and for teaching how to live right.

A word of encouragement from a teacher to a child can change a life. A word of support from a spouse can save a marriage. A word of help from a leader can inspire a person to reach her potential.

~ John C. Maxwell

Whenever I pick up a book, I'm always surrounded by loads of paper, on all sides of my desk, they tend to vary in sizes, shapes, and colors, on account of, I love to jot down a few notes every chance I get. If you were sitting next to me, you'd be laughing right now. Why? Because at whatever time I go to partake in what I happily call "Me Time," I find a comfy place and curl up. Like a Soldier of God, I have my Bible in my right hand and my book in my left hand. During all of this, I was smiling while listening to my loving husband telling our four playful sons that I'm reading; so that they should be quiet and keep away from me until my "Me Time" is over.

While all this happy madness is going on, I still got to scribble down a couple of notes and invariably look them over (is what I do), after I finish reading that breathtaking book. I even let out a few little chuckles because I tend to hear and notice our four adult sons conduct themselves like little kids at the playground (LOL). Do I get upset and close the book I was reading? No, because, I know that our four sons are just partaking of some friendly fun and I stand firmly on this Bible verse.

> Psalm 127:3-4
> 3. Yes, sons are a gift from the Lord, the fruit of the womb is a reward.
> 4. Sons born during one's youth are like arrows in a warrior's hand.

> Let parents bequeath to their children not riches, but the spirit of reverence.
>
> ~ Plato

On the flip side of all of this, when I "Finally" decide to put the book I was reading down, then I proceeded to organize my thoughts before I put them on paper. Low and behold, I suddenly experienced a series of trials and tribulations that tried to derail me from publishing this book. I'll be real with all of you because I don't believe in lying, on the contrary, God has taught me, my beloved parents and on a daily basis by my loving Gem of a husband continues to remind me always no matter what, not to lie.

> Proverbs 12:22 (ESV)
> Lying lips are an abomination to the Lord, but those who act faithfully are His delight.

> "Honesty is the best policy."
> ~ Benjamin Franklin.

Dear readers, no I haven't lost my place in the writing of this book. It's just that I'm explaining in detail what I thought before, during and when I "Finally" picked the name for this chapter.

So here I go, the days felt longer than usual, and my daily activities suddenly evolved into unexpected predicaments that gave birth to more work. Nonetheless, what almost stopped me in my tracks was when I experienced my second mild stroke on March 8, 2017. Oh yes, it caught me by surprise and hit me like a ton of bricks, too. The entire right side of my body became immediately numbered, and as for my tongue, it felt as if it weighed 300 pounds.

Conveying my feelings became difficult; nonetheless, I thank the Lord (every day of my life) for blessing me with such a vigilant husband that's 100% on track when it comes to any aspect of my life (alleluia).

> Genesis 2:24 (ESV)
> Therefore a man shall leave his father and his mother and hold fast to his wife, and they shall become one flesh.

> "Love is a vessel that contains both security and adventure, and commitment offers one of the great luxuries of the lifetime, Marriage is not the end of romance, it's the beginning."
> ~ Esther Perel

Yes, all of the above happened to me, while I was praying and decided on the name for this first chapter, which is "Finally."

Chapter Two ~ A Habitual Ritual

I begin every day with a morning praise session to the Alpha and Omega. Now, I'm not getting my praise on because it's going to be a perfectly blessed day, on the contrary (it might not be). However, I do feel a burning sensation in my bones, that if I don't recognize how grateful I am for who and what Jesus Christ has added or subtracted from my life, my day doesn't feel complete. It's so ironic, no matter what went on, in between all the chaos in my life and running around like a chicken without a head (just kidding), I can sincerely say that there was always someone or something that left a memorable mark in my mind and heart. Plus, this is why I continue to thank God every day in a praiseful manner (sometimes the neighbors can hear me) but that doesn't matter because when they see my family and me in the hallway of the building where we reside, all they do is smile.

Whoever is listening to me might be joining my morning praise routine from their apartments. On account of, everything I say is giving glory and honor to the Master Architect of my life, and He's also the inspiration to why I write.

James 1:2-4 (NLT)
2. Dears brothers and sisters, when troubles of any kind come your way, consider it an opportunity for great joy.
3. For you know that when your faith is tested, your en-

durance has a chance to grow.

4. So let it grow, for when your endurance is fully developed, you will be perfect and complete, needing nothing.

Hey, you know what? I stumbled upon this conscientious piece of advice:

> Trials teach us what we are; they dig up the soil and let us see what we are made of.
>
> ~ Charles Spurgeon

My affectionate husband, Pastor Carlos Ramon Advincola, Sr. and our four outspoken sons (they're candid, in a respectful fashion): Carlos Jr., Josue', Esteban and Elias are the fuel that continues to generate the ultimate love and power that transformed my day and life into a day without pain (thank You, Jesus).

I feel like testifying...

Once I accepted Jesus Christ as my Lord and Savior 32 ½ years ago, I've chiseled into my daily routine to acknowledge God's presence and worship in a loud and joyful way. My hubby also embraced the same method before we said "I Do" and once we got "Hitch" (that may sound funny but it has a beautiful definition) and had our four sons, we've implanted in their minds and hearts that it's a blessing to praise the Lord.

Definition Time:
The term hitch in slang or country terminology which means to unite in marriage.

> Hebrews 13:15 (WEB)
> Through Him, then, let us offer up a sacrifice of praise to God continually, that is, the fruit of lips which proclaim allegiance to his name.

Everywhere Jesus Christ opens a door for me to teach or preach His word, I'll be there, like a broken record reminding the young ladies that they should wait on the Lord when it comes to having a soul-mate (getting married).

> Psalm 27:14 (ESV)
> Wait for the Lord; be strong, and let your heart take courage; wait for the Lord!

> "Never be afraid to trust an unknown future to a known God."
>
> ~ Corrie ten Boom

> In all of my written blogs and videos, I'm always inquiring about how many couples want to get married? I ask this question regularly because so many people want to get married; but they're not ready to pray, wait, respect each other's opinions and especially learn how to forgive.

> Ecclesiastes 4:9 (ESV)
> Two are better than one because they have a good reward for their toil.

> "Marriage is an exclusive union between one man and one woman, publicly acknowledged, permanently sealed, and physically consummated."
>
> ~ Assorted Authors

Throughout these 30 years, three months and 25 days of being "happily" married to my Dominican Danish (that's one of the thousands of lovey-dovey names I call my husband). I quickly noticed the heaviness of my speech, how my tongue hung out on the right side of my mouth and as a result, my hubby jumped into action like Superman (oh yes he did). He laid his hands on me, followed by speaking over me an Old School Holy Ghost filled prayer that calmed the waters of that unexpected mild stroke (hallelujah). That's why, every time I open my eyes, all I feel like doing is thanking Jesus Christ for blessings me with such a God-fearing husband.

Ephesians 5:25 (HCSB)
Husbands, love your wives, just as Christ loved the church and gave Himself for her.

I firmly believe that my Gem of a husband is my partner for life and that's why we've instilled the following quote in our marital lives.

"The difference between an ordinary marriage is in giving just a little extra every day, as often as possible, for as long as we both shall live."
~ Fawn Weaver

1 Corinthians 13:4-7 (NCV)
4. Love is patient and kind. Love is not jealous, it does not brag, and it is not proud.
5. Love is not rude, is not selfish, and does not get upset with others. Love does not count up wrongs that have been done.
6. Love takes no pleasure in evil but rejoices over the truth.
7. Love patiently accepts all things. It always trusts, always hopes, and still endures.

Whenever I look back on what transpired on March 8, 2017, all that pokes my mind and heart (hypothetically speaking) is that I had to grab the bull by the horns, not waste any time and take advantage of every minute, hour and day that our Heavenly Father allows me to see.

Ephesians 5:16
So be careful how you act; these are difficult days. Don't be fools; be wise; make the most of every opportunity you have for doing good.

Or, in other words.

You gain strength, courage, and confidence by every experience in which you stop to look fear in the face. You can say to yourself, 'I lived through this honor. I can take the next thing that comes along.'

~ Eleanor Roosevelt

On March 21, 2017, at 10:27 AM, while my Honey Bun of a husband was working on the covers of the CD's that enclose potent messages that Christ has given him to teach and preach, and I was adding the finishing touches to this book, the Lord shared this analogy with me.

Life is like a cup of tea, at first it tastes healthy and hard to swallow; however, after you learn to sweeten it to your liking, you'll enjoy it more.

In the beginning, specific people or situations may seem a bit arduous to bear, or you might even have to lose a few nights of sleep; nonetheless, when you learn how to hand them over to Christ, what you once thought was a heavy burden to carry, can eventually turn into another one of life's lessons.

Psalm 55:22 (HCSB)
Cast your burden on the Lord, and He will sustain you.
He will never allow the righteous to be shaken.

If there is no struggle, there is no progress,

~ Frederick Douglass.

Ladies and gentlemen, at your leisure, feel free to enjoy another cup of tea with me. Take your time to sweeten it to your liking and please don't forget that I'm using tea as a metaphor for life.

I'd like to move on to the next chapter of this book. Care to join me?

Chapter Three ~ Let's be, more Vigilant?

Here's a thought, before you leave your home every day for school or work. Please, ask the Prince of Peace in prayer to place an encouraging word in your mouth and heart for someone in need. For instance, that dear bus driver, who's so polite and patient with all of his/her passengers? Who never lets a day go by without saying a morning hi. It doesn't matter whether it's raining, snowing or blazing hot outside, there's always a positive gesture coming from their direction.

Be that as it may, nobody seems to care, blink an eye or open their mouths and say "likewise." So why don't you be the one that breaks the ice and show the other passengers that common courtesy isn't extinct and I'm sure that others will follow in your footsteps?

> Proverbs 27:17
> Iron sharpens iron, and one man sharpens another.
>
> "A leader takes people where they would never go on their own."
>
> ~ Hans Finzel

Let's not forget about the cheerful mail person, who's always asking how's your wife or husband is doing, commenting on how respectful your kids are and that every time he/she sees them (your daughters or sons), they always reply by saying hello Ma'am or Sir. More than likely the mail carrier will have to walk up 2 to 3 flights of stairs because once again, the elevator isn't working. Nonetheless, during the handling of your package, you better believe that it's usually accompanied by the phrases "It's a beautiful day" or did you see Everybody Loves Raymond last night?

I'm making emphasis on this because my hubby, our four sons and I watch the news every night and it's so unfortunate to see how there's always someone attempting to commit suicide or already committed hara-kiri. As my family and I sit in front of the television or around the laptop in the living room, to hear how the family, friends or neighbors describe the man, woman or youth, who took it upon themselves to end their own lives.

While we pay close attention to the conversations between the reporters and friends, overall the crying and screaming, it left us in a state of shock, on account of how that individual felt the need to end their own life before the established time that Jesus Christ had for them. Now, during all of this, the only thought that ran through our minds was "Why would someone take their life's"? The only reply that I have to my question is "Let's be, more Vigilant"?

As my family and I continue to watch the news, it was so painful to see how the interviewed siblings and friends had tears in their eyes and kind words flowing out of their mouths when they described how loving that person was. Aside from that, didn't anyone know or notice what kind of torment that individual was experiencing? Let's be, more Vigilant? I'm going to be real, what baffles me is how nobody seemed to notice their daily structures and how specific issues were eating that person up inside. I comprehend how behind closed doors, some people tend to cry more; than in public.

People in pain tend to display a sweet and calming smile to cover up their pain. In spite of that, I still can't believe how a close friend, sibling or even a co-worker didn't notice the change in that individual. Maybe, It's Just Me, but if I see someone in pain, I'm going to jump into my inquisitorial mood immediately and subtly ask them if they need something? I'm going to be realistic; I'm going to ask more than once, especially if I see or notice that they want to vent (talk with some-one). Once again, please people, Let's be, More Vigilant?

As a happily married woman of 30 years, three months and 25 days, a mother who gave birth four awesome sons and a loving husband, who together we Pastor the most caring congregation, I feel it's my obliga-tion to at least try to come to the aid of those in need. Didn't God send His Son to do the same for you, me and the rest of society?

> John 3:16 (ESV)
> For God so loved the world, that He gave his only Son, that whoever believes in him should not perish but have eternal life.

> Forgive and give as if it were your last opportunity. Love like there's no tomorrow, and if tomorrow comes, love again.
> ~ Max Lucado

I'm going to continue watching the news with my family.

We continued listening to what the reporter had uncovered regard-ing that individual's need to kill themselves. Followed by a sudden si-lence that came over all of us and if you were standing on the other side of our apartment door, all you'd hear are these words. "Something so profound and agonizing was troubling that individual and nobody saw or felt their endless pain, and as a result, they felt the need to commit suicide. Let's be, more Vigilant?

For all we know, in their mind, suicide was the only real solution to get rid of their endless pain. All I can say is, Christ, please open our hearts and minds more; so that we can sense the anguish of our fellow man, woman, and youth, this way we can turn into (in Jesus name) a form of comfort and strengthen, in their hour of need.

> Mark 11:24 (NIV)
> Because of this, I say to you, whatever you ask for when you pray, have faith that you will receive it. Then you get it.

"We never know how God will answer our prayers, but we can expect that He will get us involved in His plan for the answer, if we are true intercessors, we must be ready to take part in God's work on behalf of the people for whom we pray."

~ Corrie ten Boom

A quick question for all of you: Who motivated that person to take their own life? Allow me to reply quickly. Was it his or her overwhelming circumstances, and as a result, the devil (who is an instigator of destruction) deceived that person into making that fatal decision. All of the above is the genesis of this.

Revelation 12:7-9
7. Now war arose in heaven, Michael and his angels fighting against the dragon. And the dragon and his angels fought back,
8. But he was defeated, and there was no longer any place for them in heaven.
9. And the great dragon was thrown down, that ancient serpent, who is called the devil and Satan, the deceiver of the whole world—he was thrown down to the earth, and his angels were thrown down with him.

Haven't you noticed that misery always loves company? It's a shame, but all so right. The devil (I rebuke him in the name of Jesus) was an angel of light in heaven; however, he wanted to be higher than God, and that's why he and his followers were cast down from heaven (Revelation 12:9).

Since then, a spirit of jealousy has descended. Or have you forgotten how Cain killed his brother Abel (Genesis 4:8)?

Definition Time:
Jealousy is as a deep resentment towards a rival's success.

Who's the founder or ultimate symbol of jealousy? Satan is because he infects anyone who gives him a spot in their minds or hearts. That's why when a member of the Body of Christ doesn't pray, study God's word on a daily basis or regularly congregates at a Church, where the true Gospel of Jesus Christ is taught they become easy prey of destruction.

> 1 Peter 5:8 (ESV)
> Be sober-minded; be watchful. Your adversary the devil prowls around like a roaring lion, seeking someone to devour.

> It is sad that today many times people give up in the hard times and never get to enjoy the fruit of all their labor.
> ~ Joyce Meyers

After numerous years of research and close observation, I feel it's crucial to stress the importance of implementing a daily prayer schedule. I say this because a large-scale of Christians of all ages, far and near have revealed to me to that they don't posit the need to pray every day. Perchance they haven't come across this Bible verse.

> 1 Peter 5:7 (ESV)
> Casting all your anxieties on Him, because he cares for you.

> "There is no other activity in life so important as that of prayer. Every other activity depends upon prayer for its best efficiency."
> ~ M.E. Andross

I don't feel the need for a cloak-and-dagger mission to concerning my opinion on prayer. Ergo, since so many Brothers and Sisters in Christ seem to overlook the significance of cultivating an intense prayer life, a heavenly commission came over me and galvanized me to present the pros and cons of establishing a stable prayer life.

Did you know that prayer is the key to firmly planting your feet on solid ground? Then make an effort to set aside some time to pray, every day.

Definition Time:
Prayer, is a spiritual act of communicating with God or a form of worship, as in supplication, thanksgiving, adoration, or confession.

What I love about praying is that the more you pray, the clearer your mind becomes when it's dealing with issues and people that do and don't benefit you. The relationship will either get closer or when you least expect, Jesus Christ will close that friendship door.

> Luke 11:9 (HCSB)
> "So I say to you, keep asking, and it will be given to you. Keep searching, and you will find. Keep knocking, and the door will be opened to you.

> "How can you find answers, if you do not ask questions?
> ~ Lailah Gifty Akita

When you set aside 30 minutes or an hour every day so that you can pour out your heart to the Lord, so much can be accomplished afterward. During that time, you'll be able to share with God the things that you're too ashamed to tell anyone else; because perhaps you feel you're going to be pre-judged or condemned by siblings or friends (before they received all the facts). That's what I call negative, judgmental assumptions, and as a Pastor, I've witnessed a lot of it. Maybe, It's Just Me, but that's why I love studying the Bible, on account of every day I learn something new and insightful to share with the world, such as this…

> Matthew 7:1 (HCSB)
> Do not judge, so that you won't be judged.

> I sincerely concur with the following quote.

> "It is the Holy Spirit's job to convict, God's job to judge and my job to love"
> ~ Billy Graham

Don't get me wrong and I'm not prejudging anyone; However, I've seen this happen many times. When a member of the Body of Christ begins to experience a decline in their spiritual lives or someone that's taking their first steps in their Christian Quest. Both types of Christians should exclude themselves from activities that can endanger their spiritual walk. Anything or anyone that disturbs your fellowship with the Lord or directs your flesh to spiritual destruction shouldn't be allowed access into your life.

Another thing, all those associates (siblings or friends) that continuously feel the need to remind you of how cool you looked when you were in the world. Or, how much fun you had when you drank till the wee hours of the night. How throwing up every time you turned around, and not being able to attend class or go to work the next day, was so silly crazy (meaning a humdinger) because of a wicked hangover that's attacking you. Now, Maybe, It's Just Me, but, I don't consider or call that fun, nor do I believe that it's the best way of drowning your sorrows, either.

In my opinion, it's another form of falsely escaping from your problems, and if you're not careful, you can even engage in other promiscuous activities that will later lead to a destructive lifestyle. In the end, all I have to say is "Lord take the wheel (please)? On that note, I could give you a long list of what I think isn't a productive use of your time; but I won't because probably you'll ignore my advice because your flesh could already be addicted to that particular activity. Followed by, I heard various people tell me that someone's trash is another person's treasure.

Would you like to escape the traps that the devil has prepared for you in order not to be easily deceived by his cunning antics? Then spend more than an hour doing something that's going to generate a spiritual explosion in your life. In other words, sink your teeth into the studying of God's word, study a chapter everyday or pick up a book that motivates you to rekindle an old spark that will lead you further into spiritual growth. If your calling is playing a musical instrument or composing a touching poem, do it for God's glory. Here's something I love to do with my handsome husband, we create delicious treats for the entire family to eat, in the comforts of our new home.

Those are only a few suggestions; but if you ask Jesus Christ in prayer, I'm sure He'll open your eyes to some more activities. On the grounds of, if you continue down that disorderly path, instead of seeking contentment or strength in the things or events that bring you closer to the Lord, you'll continue to live your life as a person that loves to waste their time.

Keep in mind, that the provocateur of wasting time is named Satan and the Apostle Paul advises us to be alert (at all times; because this was the platform of the enemy's deception).

> 2 Corinthians 11:3 (ESV)
> But I am afraid that as the serpent deceived Eve by his cunning, your thoughts will be led astray from sincere and pure devotion to Christ.

I'd like to share this quote with all of you; because it will hit a home run if it arrives at the proper time.

> "Time = life; therefore, a waste of your time and waste of your life, or master your time and master your life."
> ~ Alan Lakein

Perhaps, some of you have thought that I've lost my place or changed the subject. By the grace of God, no I haven't. I'm still connecting the dots, and I hope you are, too. Don't get me wrong, I'm not belittling anyone's suffering; however, what I am saying is that if that man, woman or youth (experiencing some pain) would have come across someone who had the charisma to lift their spirits up, with a kind word, perhaps they wouldn't come to that tragic conclusion. That's why I titled this 2nd. Chapter, Let's be, more Vigilant?

Here's a little bit of my testimony. When I came to the Lord, I carried a lot of past baggage with me. Thoughts and habits that only directed me down a path of bitterness and inflating anger. Even so, Jesus

Christ led me to a God-filled church where the congregation was full of men, women, youth that love and serve the Lord, wholeheartedly, and the complete icing on the cake was that the Pastor who's now with the Lord, (Pastor Eugenio Sankis) impacted my life, beyond words can ever say.

Every time Pastor Eugenio Sankis noticed that I was about to fall into a spiritual relapse, he'd take time out of his hectic schedule and talk to me as if I was his daughter (he was extremely vigilant). The love, respect, and concern weren't only for me; but also towards my parents and siblings, too. Pastor Sankis took the Pastoral Minister to a deep level. His biblical knowledge was thick, filled with love and patience. No matter what time it was, whether it was extremely hot or cold, he'd leave his home at 6:00 am to teach, preach, give something to eat to the homeless and even bring a person to the Church. The affliction he displayed for those lost men and women was out of this world.

For example, I was a newbie in the Lord, and Pastor Eugenio Sankis found a homeless man who was hungry, hadn't taken a bath for weeks and the clothes that homeless gentlemen had on were so filthy. Nonetheless, that didn't stop the older brothers in Christ from escorting him to the Church basement and with Pastor Sankis hands-on help, bathe the man. Whatever Pastor Sankis did, he did it with love and complete.

Pastor Sankis told his wife, Pastor Yolanda Sankis to go home and bring back one of his "good" suits, socks, under clothing and shoes for this homeless gentleman, that he just met that morning.

The generosity that Pastor Sankis displayed towards this homeless gentleman left me speechless. He received a bath, new clothes and a haircut to boot. I'm honest; if I didn't see it with my own eyes, I wouldn't have believed it.

Pastor E. Sankis always shared this Bible verse with me when he noticed that I was on the verge of a spiritual relapse.

> Matthew 11:28 (HCSB)
> "Come to Me, all of you who are weary and burdened, and I will give you rest."

"Many of life's failures are people who did not realize how close they were to success when they gave up."

~ Thomas Edison

I'd "Love" to give tribute to Pastor Eugenio Sankis, and this is why.

Romans 13:7 (HCSB)
Pay your obligations to everyone: taxes to those you owe taxes, tolls to those you owe tolls, respect to those you owe respect, and honor to those you owe honor.

A Tribute to Pastors Eugenio and Yolanda Sankis:

Beyond a shadow of a doubt, he was a True Man of God (in every sense of the word), a loving husband, concerned father and a pillar to the community. Who was Pastor Eugenio Sankis in my eyes? As I reflect on how Pastor Sankis impacted my heart and life, I feel profound gratitude which will last me for the rest of my life.

What will always stand out as the days, months and years go by, was the way he called me "Beloved" and how his lovely wife Yolanda was so aware of my every move. You see, Pastor Yolanda was a self-taught seamstress and let's be realistic, sometimes when a person willingly hands over their lives to Jesus Christ, they tend to bring along some baggage. As for me, I dressed in super short sleeves and skirts that were a bit tight and so on. However, Pastor Eugenio left the ladies dress code to his beautiful wife.

Pastor Yolanda, was a soft-spoken, sweet and blessed with a motherly kindness. Whenever she saw that my appearance wasn't that of a young lady who wanted to serve the Lord, she'd call me to the side, offer me something tasty to eat and let the Lord take the wheel. All I knew was that after that pow-wow (the talk), I felt freer than before and my past scars continued to heal in such a Heavenly way (praise the Lord).

Pastors Eugenio and Yolanda were both a little short and extremely cheerful; but when they entered a room, all you felt was love. When either of them opened their mouths, all you'd receive was the anointing of the Holy Ghost cover you (alleluia). They both lived to serve the Lord, their children, the congregation and whoever God put in their path (I say path; because they were one according to Genesis 2:24).

At the end of each service, and the Holy Spirit had finished ministering to all those in the church, Pastor E. Sankis would ring his bell as a sign of joy. Then he'd proceed to sit behind the driver's seat of the church bus and start taking everyone home. During the drive home, the Brothers and Sisters of the congregation would begin praising the Lord with testimony or Christian song, and suddenly, Holy Ghost Fire would descend over everyone that was in the Church bus. Yes, it did, and it as always something that touched my heart.

The manner in which Pastor E. Sankis rang his little red bell (that was his trademark), inside and outside of the Church. It truly brought joy to my heart. Ergo, he'd humorously ring that bell to remind everybody that Holy Ghost was touching him. Something else that brought delight to my heart was the manner in which Pastor Sankis would take the congregation to the bakery where lots of Christians from far and near, would go out of their way to purchase some of the barkery's hot, buttery bread.

The blessings didn't stop there, because Pastor E. Sankis would park the Church bus in front of my building, so he could explain to me whatever I didn't comprehend during the service, I asked tones of questions, and he'd happily answer them for God's glory. Finally, after all, was said and done, Pastor Sankis would pray so that my family would come to the Lord and that we'd all have a blissful sleep. Before I'd get out of the bus, say good-night, Pastor Sankis would ask me to pop my head out of my window; so he knew that I'd gotten upstairs safely.

I'd obey his request because that only continue to confirm how much of a husband, father and especially Man of God he was. While I was walking up those four flights of stairs, the peace of Jesus Christ continued to cover my life. I felt the need to obey, respect and give glory to the Lord for placing this Man of God in my life. He's also the key in the molding of my spiritual life. Jesus Christ never gave up on anyone, and Pastor E. Sankis was an actual example of this.

1 Corinthians 11:1 (ESV)
Be imitators of me, as I am of Christ.

Pastor E. Sankis wore the 1 Corinthians 11:1 on his sleeve, he also taught me and many others, in and out of the Body of Christ that whoever enters your life, no matter how big or small their sin is, never refuse to share the message of Jesus Christ with them. That God-fearing Couple, Pastors Sankis displayed the true meaning of a loving and caring couple, who only felt the need to feed the sheep that Jesus Christ placed in their life's (in every extension of the word). I'm a better person because of them.

Thank You, Heavenly Father for granting me the privilege of meeting, interacting and learning so much from these two remarkable individuals. I'll always value the time we spent together. Wow, walking down Memory Lane, Christian Style, breaths strength, a calming spirit and the Holy Ghost jolts my heart (hallelujah).

For those of you who are wondering where Pastor Engeuino and Yolanda Sankis are now, Pastor Engeuino has concluded his minister on earth, and now he's residing in Heaven. As for his lovely wife, Pastor Yolanda is continuing to help raise her beautiful grandbabies, helping others in every sense of the word and without a doubt, serve the Lord with love in her heart.

Now, try this before you go to sleep or leave your home every morning, pick up your Bible or download the free Bible app on your phone and choose a chapter or verse and study it every day. Look for a verse in the Bible that honestly speaks to the heart of someone in need. Then ask God in prayer to grant you a memorizing spirit; so that you can freely communicate with a loving and respectful tone to that individual. I say this because often, people in pain tend to want to argue more than listen. In all possibity, they've undergone a traumatic experience in the past or recently. Remember, that during those moments of what I call "Evangelizing Outside," I've discovered that it takes two people to argue and one person to listen. So which one do you choose to be? The one who's listens with an understanding ear or the person that rather continue quibbling about the smallest thing?

Not to mention, we're vessels of Jesus Christ, who by the Lord's love, we are sent out into the world to speak to somebody's heart and not entice them into fighting with us. Maybe, It's Just Me, but I love to cover all the bases and keep the conversation flowing for God's glory. Let's be, more Vigilant?

The Bible is packed with great verses to share with people who are slightly unbalanced, upset and dismayed about what life has in store for them.

We're soldiers, and we've been called by the Lord to assist the sick, console the wounded, lead the blind and use our testimonies as compasses to direct those in their spiritual darkness into the light that Jesus Christ offers.

> John 8:12 (ESV)
> Again Jesus spoke to them, saying, "I am the light of the world. Whoever follows me will not walk in darkness, but will have the view of life.
>
> "There is nothing more important than your eternal salvation."
> ~ Kirk Cameron

So often we forget that Jesus Christ paid a hefty price for our eternal life and instead of passing on that "Good News" to all those who feel spiritually lost, we don't administer our time wisely and as a result, we get so wrapped up in our issues. That's why we can't become oblivious to the fact that we live in a society full of people in pain.

> Philippians 2:4 (ESV)
> Let each of you look not only to his interests but also to the interests of others.
>
> One of the best ways to walk in love is to be a blessing to other people or to help them.
> ~ Joyce Meyers

As long as I live, I'll never forget about how I felt before I knocked on God's door and He let me in (Revelation 3:20). My heart was full of resentment, until that day when Christ came to my rescue. He placed someone in my path; so that I could finally see and comprehend that those tormenting issues would someday evolve into more significant blessings (thank You, Jesus).

> 1 Peter 5:10 (NCV)
> And after you suffer for a short time, God, who gives all grace, will make everything right. He will make you secure and support you and keep you from falling. He called you to share in his glory in Christ, a beauty that will continue forever.

> "Even in the greatest afflictions, we ought to testify to God, that, in receiving them from His hand, we feel pleasure in the midst of the pain, from being afflicted by Him who love."
>
> ~ John Wesley

Suicide is an extremely touchy subject that so many people are reluctant to discuss. Why? On account of so many people want to ignore the symptoms. Nonetheless, if you genuinely listen to the conversations in your neighborhood grocery stores, public schools and don't be closed minded to what I'm about to say, but in a lot of the Christian churches, too. Maybe, It's Just Me. However, my husband and I have spoken to members of the Body of Christ that refuse to increase their prayer time, they hardly open their Bibles at home, and when it comes to congregating in God's house for some Brotherly/Sisterly love and support, they don't attend. As a result, some immature Christians take this opportunity to gossip, instead of praying for them.

Church, we need more of this in today's congregations.

> Philemon 1:6 (NOG)
> As you share the faith you have in common with others,

I pray that you may come to have complete knowledge of every blessing we have in Christ.

"Happiness is only real when shared."
~ Jon Krakauer

Don't get me wrong, and I'm not ignoring what's going on around me. However, as a Pastor, I feel I must teach the Body of Christ that rebuking the devil when he attacks their finances, marriage, family structure, employment isn't a sin. Furthermore, the mind is where the enemy loves to plant his lousy seed.

Let's be, more vigilant and realistic, too. Everyone is under attack in one form or another, and the best remedy for what ails us during those trying times is the following.

James 4:7 (ESV)
Submit yourselves therefore to God. Resist the devil, and he will flee from you.

Our minds can be kept free of anxiety as we dump a load of our cares on the Lord in prayer.
~ Charles Swindoll

Please, put your phones down, stop texting for a few minutes and carefully listen to this? If you notice that a sibling, friend or co-worker isn't acting like they normally do, a bit confused, angry or only mentioning on how abandoned they feel, then try to change the conversation from a negative one and share an encouraging word with the person. By doing so, you can be the deciding factor to what they're about to do or what their next move is. Let's be, more Vigilant?

Definition Time:
Encouragement means to support, boost, lift, and endorsement with words or gestures.

Maybe, It's Just Me; but, I still tend to look back (on a daily basis) on what Jesus did for me when I didn't have Him in my life and especially when I was going through some tough times. How I felt when one day a young Christian girl named Dinelia, who cared for my loving mother, as her home attendant (34 years ago), listened to God when He told her to go and minister to a girl in pain"… That girl was me.

Sister Dinelia is an incredibly cheerful person, loves to converse and spoke with a calming tone, displayed the Lord's peace, from her head to her toes. After observing her for several days, eavesdropping on the conversations, she shared with my parents and paying close attention to her tranquil vocabulary, my outlook on life began to change. Every time Sister Dinelia opened her mouth, all that came out were loving and respectful words. She displayed a calming spirit, and that sensation came over me.

> Psalm 147:3 (ESV)
> He heals the brokenhearted and binds up they're wounds.

Dinelia and I meeting didn't occur by chance or luck; God destined it. Our encounter was ordained even before we were both born. This new found friendship was the turning point in my agonizing life, and ever since then, I'm proud to say that I'm serving the Lord with joy in my heart, a happy skip in my walk and constant praise that last for days.

> Psalm 71:8 (NOG)
> My mouth is filled with your praise, with your glory all day long.

> "In a futile attempt to erase our past, we deprive the community of our healing gift. If we conceal our wounds out of fear and shame, our inner darkness can neither be illuminated nor become a light for others."
> ~ Brennan Manning

As I type each letter, a part of my past stands right in front of me and observing how much I've allowed Jesus Christ to transform my life. I'm happier than ever, laughter is continuously overflowing in our new home, and I'm comfortable in my skin.

> Psalm 150:2 (ESV)
> Praise him for his mighty deeds; praise him according to his excellent greatness!

> "Life's not easy for anybody. The wind and the waves are right there all the time waiting to knock you over, but the point is you have to step out of the boat anyway. You have to trust God enough, to believe that He sees the bigger picture and would never let the wind and the waves get the better of you."
>
> ~ Staci Stallings,

Dinelia was born and raised in Puerto Rico, where she resided with her mother, father, sisters, brothers and lots of nieces and nephews, too. They're an extremely tight-knit family who loves the Lord.

Let me share a loving and more profound story about my Spiritual Mother, Pastor Dinelia Peguero. That's correct, she's my Spiritual Mother and is Pastoring a Church with her loving husband. She's been happily married 31 years to the love of her life, Pastor Negron Diaz Peguero, they have given birth to 1 daughter, Danelis Mercado Peguero, two sons Evangelist Gilberto Peguero, and the youngest is Rafael Peguero. In the grandbaby department Pastors, Negron and Dinelia has various grandchildren.

I'm so grateful and honored to say that when I needed words of comfort, Pastor Dinelia Peguero set aside her daily routine and allowed herself to become the vessel of hope, love and Spiritual Fortress that I truly needed. She will always have a special place in my heart, and yes, she was more than vigilant concerning my needs.

No, no, no, I haven't lost my train of thought (hehe). It's just that if a person has positively impacted your life, you should display some gratitude towards them. Because if you pass them by as if you didn't obtain any insight from them, you're conducting yourself as an ungrateful individual. And I believe that is not who you are.

Moving right along and yes I can definitely say that I was financially stable, lived in a beautiful home with two loving parents who didn't think twice about going days without eating and working long hours so that my siblings and I would have a roof over our heads, food in our tummies and clothes on our backs.

I am the 2nd. person in my family to graduate from college and whenever I had homework to do or studying for a test, my Mommy would sit by my side all night. Why do you ask? Well, I'm going to be more than honest. My family and I lived in a massive apartment on Fordham Road in the Bronx, the neighbors were friendly, but what troubled me the most was that every time I had to do some school work, an unwelcome mouse that lived in our house (stop laughing), and he'd pop out and scare me. I can laugh now, but back then I was always so frightened to sit down at the dinner table because I always knew that Ben the mouse (that's right, I named him) would come out of his hiding place.

From afar, I looked like a together person, blessed with concerned parents and siblings that would cut out their arm for each other and educational wise; I was on my way to a prosperous future. However, I still felt that something was missing in my life. All in all, the King of Kings blessed me with two determined parents that tried to move any mountain so that I could obtain peace of mind. They were more than vigilant, but what I was experiencing was spiritual and not carnal. But, they didn't comprehend; because they weren't Christian yet. Yes, they witnessed my everyday struggles; however, they didn't understand what was going on with me or couldn't see it. Nonetheless, they tried to be more vigilant, everyday.

That's what I call "Old School Parenting," and I'm going to say something that a lot of people might not agree with me, but that's why Jesus Christ blessed everyone with their own opinion. In other words, don't be afraid to agree to disagree.

Definition Time:

Parenting, the rearing of children.

Rearing is to take care, support financial wise until they can support themselves and offer mightful advice when needed.

If you merge both words, you'll notice that not much of this is occurring in today's society. Follow me closely, please? I'm not telling you how to live your life or raise your children. What I am suggesting is that if parents would invest more time in their bundles of Joy (their children), today's youth wouldn't be running wild in the streets. I'd like to pass on to all of you the same mindful wisdom my parents and in-laws bestowed upon me.

For example, if you have bills to pay and children to feed, then do it and don't misuse your money. Why are you spending your money on items or going to places that only benefit "your flesh" and leave your family up the creek without a paddle?

If your married and your spouse doesn't want to accompany you because he or she knows that where you'd like to go won't benefit any of you, then why go? You haven't paid the rent, purchased food for the week and the laundry hasn't been washed, so why aren't you administering your cash better?

When it comes to Parent Teacher Conference, you don't attend, your constantly busy getting ready to go out with undesirable friends, instead of taking care of your family. However, if another child looks at your daughter or son the wrong way, you rush into the school like a herd of buffalo.

Probably some or most of you are saying right now, I'm young, it's my life and money and "nobody" has to tell me what to do with it. Now, my reply to this, you are right, but remember you're a parent, and your children should come first. It's unfortunate, but someone can come to an unpleasant conclusion and then the entire family suffers.

Going back to the financial situation, of course, it's your money and life, and you can do with it what you desire. However, if you continue at the rate you're going, someone might brand you as an unfit parent. Then so many other issues will be uncovered. For instance, your age, your living conditions, and 2 or 3 neighbors might even dare to discuss your parenting skills with specific agencies.

I go into depth with the manner in which some people may perceive your parenting skills; because it's a shame; but not everyone is truthful to discuss what they think or feel. I continue to make emphasis on this manner; because when I was growing up, neighbors weren't just neighborhoods, they were an extension of the family. If you didn't have dinner for your babies, the next door neighbor would come to your family's rescue without any hesitation. As a child, my community believed in the phrase "One for All and All for One." That's the motto of the Three Musketeers, and that's the way my community conducted themselves (those were the days). Oh yes, please let's be, more vigilant, but in a mindful way?

Yes, I'm a wife, mother of four, Pastor; but I'm also a realistic too.

A Tribute to Leticia Scott
(My Courageous Biological Sister)

When it came to my siblings, I had a sister and her name was Leticia, she too has gone home to be with the Lord. What can I say about Letty, that was her loving nickname at home? Well, Letty was beautiful, funny, knowledgeable in so many areas, and had no problem putting people in their place, when she saw that some type of abuse was about to take place. She was my older sister, we slept in the same bed, held hands all night, and she knew just what to say to make my day.

Of course, everything wasn't ice cream and cake with us all the time; but no matter what went on between us, I knew that she was always in my corner and I was in her's. Letty was night, and I was the day, she was extremely friendly, and I was reticent; however, we were sisters to the end. I am so proud of Letty's achievements, and she applauded mine. We were an odd team, full of love that overflowed till the day she went home with the Lord.

When it was time for Letty to wed, I couldn't be anything but happy for her because the man she married was so loving and caring, his name was John Robert Scott. The Lord allowed Letty to bless our family with a son named Deshun N. Scott and a daughter named Mia Divine Edwards. God bless them both, they're now all grown up, with children of their own. Mia has two sweet sons named Gregory and AJ. Now, Deshun aka El Nene is happily married and has two beautiful daughters and one handsome son. God has indeed been kind to them.

God granted my husband and I the gift of praying over my sister Leticia the day before she went home to be with the Lord. While my mother, husband and I were at the hospital, visiting my sister, our Heavenly Father prepared that day. We all laughed like babies, cried with a liberating strengthen and hugged each other as if we knew that it was the last time we'd be together. The next day a representative from the Hospital called my Mom and informed her that Letty had passed. When we inquired about my sister's last hours, the nurse told us this.

The nurse asked Letty if she is ready to go to the Calvary Hospital in a few days and my sister replied by saying that she wasn't going to Calvary Hospital; because she was going to a better place, then Leticia smiled. The nurse proceeded to visit her other patients, and when she returned to my sister's room, Letty had a huge smile and her face. The nurse said that my sister's face displayed a Heavenly peace that brought tears to the nurse's eyes (Thank You Jesus).

Since God is the vine and we're His branches (John 15:1), the outcome of whatever we do is always going to be great (especially when following Jesus Christ's footsteps). Therefore, shouldn't we always work together? I'm asking you this question at 5:11 AM, where everyone in my home is happily tucked in their beds and partaking of a blissful night's sleep. On account of, today's going to be a busy Wednesday for them at school (college), work and even Church; nonetheless, I'm still up; because of this loving fact.

> 1 John 4:19 (ESV)
> We love because he first loved us.

On that note, let's try to do more of this today.

You can communicate best when you first listen.
~ Catherine Pulsifer

My journey hasn't concluded yet, on the contrary, I'm just getting warmed up. If you're like me, you'll need another cup of tea. You know something? Yesterday my husband brought home a box of peach tea, and it's delicious. Care to join me?

Onward, fellow readers and don't forget the tea, please?

Chapter Four ~ It's a Process

Once again, it's sharing time. I'm not accustomed to sharing my secrets with everyone, but I trust all of you. Therefore, let's keep what I'm about to say just between us, okay? It goes like this, where there's joy, occasional tears will be shed. Followed by, those siblings and friends who once applauded your victories might be the first to criticize you as you start to grow spiritually. It's going to hurt and eventually you might get a little hot under the collar, too. It's only natural, and I'd like you to remember this anyway...

> Romans 12:21 (ISV)
> Do not be conquered by evil, but overcome evil with good.

> "I hope that real love and truth are stronger in the end than any evil or misfortune in the world."
> ~ Charles Dickens

Care to deliberate on this? Note that getting hysterical, placing blame upon yourself or others isn't the way out of any predicament. It doesn't bring a solution either, on the contrary, it only delays the process of accepting the fact that you're at a point in your life, where you're encountering something unpleasant, hard to handle and your flesh refuses to accept the fact that God will eventually offer you a way out of that mess.

Mull over this? Why don't you focus attention on the transformation of a caterpillar to a butterfly? Here are a few steps that a caterpillar has to embark upon to embrace the form of a beautiful butterfly. It's called the metamorphosis stage.

The caterpillar chooses a place which it can hang like a tree branch. It covers itself up with its saliva and forms a shell-like cover. This procedure is called a cocooning, and it starts to digest itself into a slimy liquid. In this liquid, a few cells begin the process of forming the body parts. The remaining liquid is used as the food until the butterfly fully grows. Once the caterpillar comes out of the cocoon, it unleashes its colorful beauty upon the world.

I get it when it comes to the Law of Repetition, the Bible perpetually uses it, when it wants to drill a particular fact in your minds and hearts. Please, stop repeating to yourself that the situation you're currently in will never pass or get better. Besides you're allowing yourself to believe and see that your case is more prominent than what it is. The Bible is full of remarkable facts regarding how things will pass or die, in Jesus name.

> 2 Corinthians 1:3-4 (ESV)
> 3. Blessed be the God and Father of our Lord Jesus Christ, the Father of mercies and God of all comfort,
> 4. Who comforts us in all our affliction, so that we may be able to comfort those who are in any affiliation, with the ease with which we are comforted by God.

> "Jesus tends to his people individually. He sees to our needs. We all receive Jesus from touching. We experience his care."
> ~ Max Lucado

> Matthew 7:7-8 (TLB)
> 7. Ask, and you will be given what you ask for. Seek, and you will find. Knock, and the door will be opened.
> 8. For everyone who asks, receives. Anyone who seeks

finds. If only you will knock, the door will open.

"What do you have that the Lord didn't provide? What do you need that the Lord can't deliver?
~ Lailah Gifty Akita

I say this from experience when you double up on your prayer time; your spiritual vision becomes much clearer. Followed by, the flesh doesn't manifest its worldly desires, and your spiritual life escalates, too. Remember, it's a process, and Jesus Christ will help you perceive the attacks of the enemy more. Once again, it's a process.

1 Peter 5:8 (MEV)
Be sober and watchful, because your adversary the devil walks around like a roaring lion, seeking whom he may devour.

"We must be alert, our eyes must be opened, and our ears must be very attentive."
~ Sunday Adelaja

Thus, increase your prayer time, get to know the God you serve more by studying His word and you'll see that there is a light at the end of that long and exasperating tunnel. Program your mind (I know you're not a robot); but try to focus your attention more on Jesus Christ, the son of God and less on the ups and downs of life. Yes, it's a process.

Probably, you're telling yourself that you're in tune enough with the Lord already, but 32 ½ years of dedicating my life to the Highest has granted me the blessing to see more than my share of Ministers of God who've said bye-bye to the noble path of serving the Lord. And have embraced the desires of the flesh as if they never had an encounter with Jesus Christ. Have they regretted it? Yes, they have, however, something was lacking in their spiritual life and that's why they turned their backs on the I Am. Dear readers, I'm not judging anyone (Matthew 7:1) because I wouldn't want anyone to attack me during my moment of agony. Nonetheless, I am offering a piece of mindful advice; so that the devil doesn't disrupt your life.

Pre-judging a person won't comfort them, instead, it will add more gasoline to the devil's dirty deeds.

My intention isn't to inject venom into your minds or hearts. However, I have an obligation to the King of Kings to educate or re-educate those of you who aren't well-informed regarding this type of subject or other topics that are equivalent to this one. What I'm about to say is sad, but it's also a harsh fact about life and so that you don't become the type of individual that refuses to maintain a healthy and balanced prayer life, ponder this?

Be extremely careful and ensure your daily responsibilities doesn't drain you or keep you so occupied and as a result, you overlook the importance of praying, because prayer is an essential ingredient for a victorious Christian life.

> Matthew 26:41 (ESV)
> Watch and pray that you may not enter into temptation. The spirit indeed is willing, but the flesh is weak."

> "Better shun the bait, than struggle in the snare."
> ~ John Dryden

It's just a tedious process (I'm not going to lie) that if you allow it, can also form healthy bones and a healthy mindset because a real captain doesn't abandon his/her ship in the midst of a massive storm. Just keep in mind, that your about to walk into a new season full of blossoming fruit that Christ had planted for you, even before you were born.

> Romans 8:18 (NCV)
> The sufferings we have now are nothing compared to the great glory that will be shown to us.

> "The more you pray, the less you'll panic. The more

you worship, the less you worry. You'll feel more patient and less pressured."

~ Rick Warren

For that reason, let's honestly be one Body of Christ and lift up the hands of those that are undergoing those terrible attacks created by the enemy. Because by doing so, we will grow more like a family, if we display a greater love for those who are unsaved and we also begin to teach this world full of needless activities that Jesus Christ, the Son of God has a plan for their life.

> When you're about to reach a goal, there are always numerous vicissitudes standing in front of you; however, if you allow Jesus Christ to be the core of your life, everything will come out smelling like a rose. It just takes a little more time than you expected.
>
> ~ Pastor Nancy Advincola

It's a process.

Flipping the page and smiling along the way (always, for God's glory).

Chapter Five ~ Jealousy and Envy

Can you be so kind as to grab your sword (Bible) and read Genesis Chapter 37, which is titled Joseph's Dreams? Before I go any further, I'd like to announce that on June 1, 2017, I'll be celebrating 31 wonderful years of serving the Lord. Every time I share something this emotional, tears automatically roll down my face, and it's because of everything Jesus Christ has done in my life has been fabulous.

> Psalm 118:1 (NLT)
> Give thanks to the Lord, for He is good! His faithful love endures forever.

> "The more you feed your mind with positive thoughts, the more you can attract great things into your life."
> ~ Roy T. Bennett

For those siblings and friends, who truly know me, they don't ask why I cry; because they comprehend that the Good Shepherd has descended over me the blessings of being a wife, mother, and Pastor. Ever since I've freely given my life to Jesus Christ, I've tried to evaluate things more, followed by engaging in events that honor this Bible verse.

Psalm 19:14 (NIV)
May these words of my mouth and this meditation of my heart be pleasing in your sights, Lord, my Rock and my Redeemer.

"Let us never forget to pray. God lives. He is near. He is real. He is not only aware of us but cares for us. He is our Father. He is accessible to all who will seek Him."
~ Gordon B. Hinckley

I've studied this story numerous times, and every time I realize how much God is speaking to me. Joseph was the youngest of 12 brothers, now, the eyes of his 11 brothers were full of envy, on account of Joseph was the son Israel procreated in his old age and as a result, Israel made Joseph a colorful robe (Genesis 37:3). In Joseph's brother's eyes and minds, Israel was esteeming Joseph more, and that festered in his 11 brothers a hateful spirit against Joseph (Genesis 37:4). Generally speaking, that's what I call "The Green-Eyed Monster Syndrome" which feast upon jealousy and envy.

Definition Time:
Envy - A feeling of discontent or covetousness about another's advantages, success, possessions, etc.

Society tends to dismiss this from their minds.

James 3:16 (ESV)
For where jealousy and selfish ambition exist, there will be disorder and every vile practice.

This quote is somewhat amusing; but all so right if you sit down and ponder each word.

"If the grass is greener on the other side of the fence, you can bet the water bill is higher."
~ Debbie Macomber

Wait a minute, before I go any further? I'd like to ask you something, now remember, honesty is the best policy? How many of you have walked in Joseph's shoes? You know what I mean. People were jealous of you because you're a talented individual. You've reached a level either spiritually or educational wise, due to your faith in the Lord of Lords and hard work, too. You have a particular gift, and as a result, you tend to stand out in any crowd.

That was the case with Joseph; he was respectful, obedient to his father's wishes and conscientious when it came to his chores, which was taking care of the flock (Genesis 37:2) without any fuse. Although, Joseph had to give his father a wrong report regarding his brother's behavior (Genesis 37:3). Joseph was 17 years old (Genesis 37:2). Israel loved Joseph more than his other 11 sons and made Joseph a colorful robe (Genesis 37:2). Now, his brothers noticed that Israel loved Joseph more and as a result, they spoke to him in a bitter manner (Genesis 37:4).

Dear body of Christ, why do you pray? Stop and think about this question before you answer it? My husband and I have served the Lord for 30 something years, and we pray so that we can maintain a healthy marriage, ministry and be an example for our four sons.

What I'm about to say may sound harsh, but it's the truth. From cold Christians to backsliders and those who've never allowed the Lamb of God to enter their lives ask my husband, Pastor Carlos Ramon Advincola, Sr. and me to pray for a particular need; but when we looked into their eyes, all we saw was anger and a desire to destroy someone.

Our reply was before we join you on your prayer quest, we'd like to know the reason why you want us to pray for you? Most refused to reply, others just laughed and the ones who were full of rage, just said; because I want my wife or husband to leave me or die. The first time, we were shocked; but we still asked why? The person's response was because they're no longer in love with their spouse.

If you're not busy, can you keep your eye on what Joseph is experiencing with his 11 jealous brothers (Genesis 37:11)? Plus, they're conspiring to kill him (Genesis 37:18), and from afar, they nicknamed him "The Dreamer" (Genesis 37:19). I'm an overly observant person and what I see ensure people's eyes is not appealing and pleasing to the Lord or humanity either.

Jealousy and envy can turn a loving person (sibling, friend or co-worker) into an angry and lunatic person, with a perpetual goal to introduce sorrow and pain into the life of the person they're choosing. Joseph was on his 11 brother's radar, and that's why they attempted to put an end to his life, by tossing him in a pit and expecting an animal to eat him (Genesis 37:19-20).

> Galatians 5:26 (ESV)
> Let us not become conceited, provoking one another, envying one another.

> "Often those that criticise others reveal what he."
> ~ Shannon L. Alder

In your lifetime, you're probably going to meet someone who desires to have the same or similar outlook of life like you. Not because you're advertising the success of your life; on the contrary, it's because something inside of you shines beyond words can describe, and that seems to keep them up at night (in a negative way). However, this is what's rolling around in the minds and hearts of Joseph's envious brothers.

> Proverbs 6:34 (ESV)
> For jealousy makes a man furious, and he will not spare when he takes revenge.

> "Envy is the art of counting the other fellow's blessings instead of your own: "
> ~ Harold Coffin.

Envy was stirring up in the minds and hearts of Joseph 11 brothers. All through this book, I've been asking you, dear readers questions because I want to keep you alert and awake. How many of you have been the source of someone's jealousy? Bear in mind; I'm not saying that you provoked it, what I'm trying to share with all of you is how someone can get upset at what Jesus Christ is doing or about to do in your life and sometimes you don't know it.

Joseph had a dream, and when he shared it with his brothers, they became even more annoyed with him (Genesis 37:5). These things develop when you innocently share something with a person or people that aren't at the same "Spiritual Level" as you. Rather than rejoicing in your victory, they turn into vicious animals, contemplating and waiting to attack you in some way.

Grant me the opportunity to be even more specific regarding Joseph's dreams. Israel immediately got a bit upset and also rebuked Joseph; because he didn't want to believe in Joseph's 2nd. Dream (Genesis 37:10). It's a shame how Joseph thought that his father would have reacted to his dreams differently. I know that I'm not the only one, that has informed someone of something so spiritual and instead of that person feeling honored that you've told them that, they turn around and refuse to recognize your real potential. What does that mean? It just symbolized that you're probably in the same boat as Joseph.

> 1 Peter 2:1 (NCV)
> So then, rid yourselves of all evil, all lying, hypocrisy, jealousy, and evil speech.

> "Insecure people only eclipse your sun because they're jealous of your daylight and tired of their dark, starless nights."
> ~ Shannon L. Aidar

That's why I always advise that people should become more cautious when it comes to informing anyone of something that contains such a powerful message. They should ask Jesus the Mediator of our lives if it will benefit that individual or not. Why do you ask Christ first? Maybe, It's Just Me, but a few nights ago, a Sister in Christ that my family and I know and love called me at about 12:00 AM to ask me how I was doing, minister wise? However before, I could get a word in edgewise, she started telling me about all the activities she was partaking of, for God's glory. I was so thrilled for her because she has been having a rough time, in every aspect of her life. Such as, she recently experienced a painful divorce (after 17 years of marriage), her son and daughter have become rebellious, her daughter also wed and then divorced at such a young age. Plus, her health is spiraling downhill fast. I felt the depths of her pain in such a way that all I could do is think and pray.

Then she asked me what was going on in my life, besides being a wife, mother, and Pastor, too? I then replied that I was at the moment of putting a finishing touch on the book you're currently reading. What happened next left me in shock. She told me she had another phone call and that she'd get back to me in 2 minutes. It's a shame to say, but I'm still awaiting her phone call. It's been more than a month since we last spoke, but still praying for her even though I sensed her jealousy while we were chatting on the phone.

> 1 John 2:9 (ESV)
> Whoever says he is in the light and hates his brother is still in darkness.

> "Jealousy blurs the focus."
> ~ Toba Beta

Going back to Joseph's ordeal, even though Israel had rebuked Joseph on account of, his dream (Genesis 37:10) and kept in his mind what Joseph discussed with him regarding the vision, Israel still sent Joseph to Shechem, upon his father's request and to see how his 11 brothers were tending to the flock (Genesis 37:12). Since Joseph was obedient and respectful, towards his father's request, he did what Israel asked (Genesis 37:14). Occasionally, these qualities that Joseph has (respect and obedience) can turn into a sword of two edges.

Joseph knew he was in hot water with his 11 brothers because of the loving relationship he shared with his father. Still, that didn't stop him from obeying his dad's wishes. That's what usually happens to so many of us when we obey what the Almighty God says, and somebody always tends to get upset. It's a struggle that everyone has when they choose to follow Christ.

When the devil tosses in your path people who attempt to discourage you, pray for them and try not to allow anyone to derail you from your calling? Amen.

Chapter Six ~ Windows

One evening, while my Love Boat of a hubby and our four sweet sons were sleeping, I perpetually asked God in prayer for the title of the 6th chapter of this book. When low and behold, I heard in a repeated fashion the Lord say the word Windows 3 times. Once again, Jesus Christ came to my rescue like a Superhero. He indeed is in my eyes. And after that, I quickly fell into a blissful sleep, like a baby (hehe). The next morning I took a few minutes to contemplate the definition of the word window.

Definition Time
Window ~ An opening in the wall of a building, the side of a vehicle, etc. for the admission of air or light, or both, commonly fitted with a frame in which are set movable sashes containing panes of glasses.

Question for all of you! What comes to your minds when you hear the word window? I've already shared my definition with all of you, and now it's your turn. Another perception I have about the word window is the following. You can compare your notes and replies with your spouse, friends or next door neighbor, if you so desire. Perhaps, it can turn into a tasty conversation during breakfast, lunch or dinner.

I have a habit of taking a mental walk down memory lane and here is one of my favorite moments. During my adolescent years, I do laugh (in a curious manner) because on my way to and from elementary school, I always noticed how some parents (mothers or fathers) would be looking out of their windows with a smile on their faces, on account of, they were awaiting the return of the bundles of joy (daughters or sons) from school.

Most people would focus their attention on shapes, sizes, or colors of the curtains hanging from the windows. But for me, my eyes always met with the eyes of those mommies, daddies and sometimes even the grandparents, who were conserving with each other about how much they miss their kids. Occasionally, I'd slow down my pace so that I could overhear their conversations; but my Mom would grab my hand and say hurry up, or we'll be late. At such a young age, I was amazed by the attentiveness those adults displayed towards their kids. My mother's daily routine was to laugh, grab my hand and ask me to please walk a little faster because if I didn't, I wouldn't receive a certificate for perfect attendance at the end of the school year.

As soon as the school clock reached 2:50 in the afternoon, my classmates and I would start to collect all our belongings because within 5 minutes those school bells would ring and all the classroom doors would fly open immediately... giving happy students the green light to go home. Friendly teachers remind their students to get home safe and to do homework before they go to bed.

Playfully running down the streets, while swinging those exciting book bags back-and-forth. Why were my classmates and I in a rush to get home? It's because we all wanted to get back before it's time for The Flintstones on television. With cartoon fever on their minds and loud laughter in our homes, afternoon fun went into effect in every house in our community. You know what? Everyone's sitting around the kitchen table, nibbling on all those tasty homemade snacks that Mom or Dad made early that day. At least that's what was going on in my home and also in a few of my friends. But during all of the above, the $1,000.00 question (did you do your homework yet) was asked, by my parents?

Ephesians 6:1-3 (NCV)
1. Children, obey your parents as the Lord wants because this is the right thing to do.
2. The command says, "Honor your father and mother." This is the first command that has a promise with it
3. "Then everything will be well with you, and you will have a long life on the earth."

Let parents bequeath to their children not riches, but the spirit of the reverence.

~ Plato

You see, I lived in a community where everyone treated each other like family. The residents looked out for each other, and when a mother, father or a grandparent had a vital appointment of some sort, the neighbor next door or somewhere in the building would attend to the child or children until their parents returned. That's what I call a friend, neighbor, and extended family.

Proverbs 27:17 (ESV)
Iron sharpens iron, and one man sharpens another.

Friends are the siblings God never gave us.

~ Mencius

Reflect on this. When I say care for your neighbor's little girl or boy, dig deep in your heart before you reply.

I mean "Old School" care, which means this:

If your children are eating dinner, the child you're caring for until the parents or guardians returns should also join in the dinner feast. Furthermore, if the children you're baby sitting have homework; but don't know how to do it, a thoughtful neighbor comes to aid and helps the child with their homework. In conclusion, if the neighbor was expecting another baby and they don't have siblings nearby or willing to care for the oldest child, a good neighbor/friend would voluntarily say "You can leave them at my house till you give birth and return home.

All through my childhood, my parents had this saying.

Where a family of 5 eat, there's always room for 1, 2 or 3 more to partake of something made with love.

Our income was that of a middle-class family, but none of us ever went to bed on an empty stomach. We were also blessed to have a roof over our heads, clean clothes on our backs and primarily two loving parents that went to bat for us every chance they get. All of us witnessed their "True Love."

When I share my childhood stories with my husband and our four sons, I can honestly see how blessed I was and still am. Even now, while I continue to think about specific events that occurred during my childhood, a smile begins to form on my face, and my heart blissfully beats more.

I'm grateful a thousand times more; because Jesus Christ blessed me with caring siblings and two loving and responsible parents. I can genuinely describe my parents as the ones who carried financial loads in such a graceful way, that most parents would have tossed in the towel at the first crisis. I thank the Lord every day, because everything that my Mommy and Papi did for my siblings, and I came from the heart. Oh, how I miss them; but I am so elated to know they're no long-suffering or worrying. Instead, they're doing this.

> Revelation 14:13 (ESV)
> And I heard a voice from heaven saying, "Write this: Blessed are the dead who die in the Lord from now on." "Blessed indeed," says the Spirit, "that they may rest from their labors, for their deeds follow them!'

Every day, when my brothers, sisters and I returned from school, I can still hear the endless laughter of a happy house full of six kids and two hard-working parents. The kitchen table covered with chicken noodle soup, ham and cheese sandwiches and the icing on the cake with a glass of milk or sweet cherry Kool-Aid. Boy, those were the "The Good Old Days." When my siblings and neighbors visited my parents home, the first thing they commented on was that no matter what was going on in the neighborhood, our home gave way to an atmosphere that was overflowing with love. Everyone went to bed with a clear conscience and a forgiving heart. The words "I'm sorry" were said with love and respect, and believe it or not, nobody went to sleep angry.

Now and then, I tend to shed tears of gratitude, on account of, I'm inclined to relive all those childhood memories. But nowadays, people don't want to trust each other, when you knock on a neighbors door, the greeting you received isn't like when my husband and I were kids. I'll continue praying to my Heavenly Father so that a spirit of true friendship, can descend in every neighborhood.

You know what? I have faith that society will someday partake of the following Bible verse.

> Hebrews 11:1 (ESV)
> Now faith is the assurance of things hoped for, the conviction of the whole of things not seen.
>
> Faith is taking the first step even when you don't see the whole staircases.
> ~ Martin Luther King, Jr.

I'm so thankful that time, sorrow and the people that Jesus Christ placed and removed from my life allowed me to learn this lesson.

> The things that make us the happiest are usually right in front of our faces, but we stop noticing those things after a while. Today is a great day to start seeing them again.
> ~ Unknown Author
>
> Ephesians 5:20 (TLB)
> Always give thanks for everything to our God and Father in the name of our Lord Jesus.

I'd like to offer you a bit of advice before I move on to the next chapter. Please, don't live your life in a rut, doing the same thing day after day, going to school or work and never getting to know your neighbor at lunchtime? Invite them over for a cup of coffee, tea, or a glass of lemon aid. If they have kids like you, perhaps both of them can become buddies for life or even say "I Do" to each other. Only God knows the future.

I firmly believe that if the Lord put you in a particular community, neighborhood or building, it's because the Alpha and Omega wants you to impact someone's life, Maybe, It's Just Me. However, you might make a difference or come to the aid of someone in need.

> Matthew 5:16 (NCV)
> In the same way, you should be a light for other people. Live so that they will see the good things you do and will praise your Father in heaven.

> Constant kindness can accomplish much. As the sun makes ice melt, kindness causes misunderstanding, mistrust, and hostility to evaporate.
> ~ Albert Schweitzer

> Proverbs 16:24 (NLV)
> Pleasing words are like honey. They are sweet to the soul and healing to the bones

> Onward, in Jesus name everyone.

> "That's what makes it so right. Your eyes—your soul is there, but the rest of you is still so undefined. That's the beauty of childhood. The eyes show everything you've seen so far, but the rest of you is still so open to possibility, to whatever you might become."
> ~ Bree Despain

Chapter Seven ~ Hidden Treasures

Everyone has a hidden gem of some sort bottled up inside of them. Whether you know it or not, decide on manifesting it in public or concealing them, till further notice. It all depends on the person and what motivates them. For instance, there are men, women, and youth (of all ages) that when they sing, whoever is feeling ill or depressed, receives immediate healing, now (that's a gift from God). Besides, to those individuals that have an artistic gene. For example, when they pick up a paintbrush, whatever they paint turns into an instant masterpiece (within a blink of an eye). On that note, I believe this.

> 1 Peter 4:10 (NCV)
> Each of you has received a gift to use to serve others.
> Be good servants of God's various gifts of grace.

> "Everyone talent God has hidden in you is not for your consumption; they are for other people's liberation."
> ~ Martin Luther King, Jr.

As I sit and reminisce about my childhood, no matter what was going on in my life, I'd look for a nook at my house or school and then proceed to grab hold of my trusty two friends (pen and pad), then I'd breathe life into whatever was roaming in my mind.

Words and thoughts would continuously flow in and out of my mouth, but the word of the Lord smoothens my mind and heart.

~ Pastor Nancy Advincola

Psalm 119:50
This is my comfort in my affliction that your promise gives me life.

Just like a teacher doesn't leave his/her home without their lesson plans or the papers they graded the night before, I couldn't dream of stepping one foot outside of my apartment without a bag full of pens (I preferred the color blue) and a thick notebook to boot. For some reason, wherever I look at, something always seems to catch my eye, followed by awakening those creative juices that keep me up all night.

My mind tends to shift gears and organize all the thoughts that are rolling around in my mind. But before this process comes to an end, I have jotted down a few notes for God's glory and my peace of mind.

I'm always asked by siblings and friends why I love to write? My only reply was and still is that all I see on television or read on the internet in various books and sites are stories about heartache, murder, suicide and lots of unpleasantness. I'm well-aware that often that's what going on in a person's life; even so, I'm an optimistic person that believes in "Happy Endings" (don't you)?

Here's another reason I love to write.

John 14:27 (NLV)
Peace I leave with you. My peace I give to you. I do not give peace to you as the world gives. Do not let your hearts be troubled or afraid.

Faith is a leap without asking any questions and eventually landing in a safe place.

~ Pastor Nancy Advincola

I'm not refusing to accept the events that go on around me; however, deep down inside of my heart, I can't stop praying because I want our Heavenly Father to offer that person, couple or family a way out of their dilemma (for real).

All I can do when someone in pain is to remind them of this...

> Matthew 5:4 (ESV)
> Blessed are those who mourn, for they shall be comforted.
>
> "Sometimes, the best way to help someone is just to be near them."
>
> ~ Veronica Roth

My life is about to venture into new waters, and it's such a treat to know that all of you are joining me on this phenomenal writing journey. However, as you all know, excursions vary in many ways, and that's why I'm going to bring this quote along with me.

> If I can stop one heart from breaking, I shall not live in vain; if I can ease one life the aching, or cool one pain, I shall not live in vain.
>
> ~ Emily Dickinson,

While I was typing, I could feel some sweet Jesus Joy cover me from the head to my toes. On that note, it's time to testify about Jesus Christ, and I'm consistently doing it with a huge smile, a playful skip in my step and endless praise for what the Lord continues to do for my family and my life. Once again, I'll joyfully say "Hallelujah."

Therefore, whatever the Lord places in your heart and mind to do, embrace it and share with the world your God Given Gift.

Keep this in mind.

> Isaiah 64:8 (ESV)
> But now, O Lord, you are our Father; we are the clay, and you are our potter we are all the work of your hand.

"Believe in yourself. You are braver than you think, more talented than you know, and capable of more than you imagine.

~ Roy T. Bennett

Chapter Eight ~ The Wonder Years

Here, I'm going to share with all of you how similiar the comedy-drama that ran on ABC from 1988 through 1993, was almost like my life. Starring Fred Savage, Danica Mckellar, and other talented cast members. Grant me a few minutes so that I can give you a short; but sweet summary of this show, if you've never seen this show? The Wonder Years main focus was on the relationships of a loving and hard working family and how the community dealt with life's issues.

The main character was an odd 12 years old boy named Kevin Arnolds. Now Kevin lived in the suburbs, surrounded by his family and friends, it's touching adventures and the impact they left on everyone. What my husband and I loved about the show was how Kevin narrated each story. The issues they addressed were real and always touched a special place in our hearts.

Our family couldn't go to sleep until we watched the daily episode; because it openly discussed the issues that so many teens were facing. The funny and sweet part about this program was the manner in which the Arnold family dealt with day to day concerns (that's why they were worth watching).

I felt right at home with The Wonder Years because the father (Dan Lauria) and the mother (Alley Mills) both had a distinctive way of handling the concerns of life, family, and finances (they reminded me of my Papi & Mami). The dad wasn't much of a talker, but he got the job done (just like my father). While on the other hand, the mother was so detailed in everything she said, once again (just like my mother). After the Lord called my parents to His presence, I watched "The Wonder Years" as if the producers were talking about my family.

It goes to show you that opposites do attract and that's what made the show so entertaining. Don't get me wrong. I'm not saying that one parent's method was superior to the other, but what I am saying is that they're just different; however, there still covered with honesty and love (how great is that)? Instead of seeing Fred Savage and his family, I saw my family and me.

You see, my father was a merchant marine, and he had been all over the world; but when it came to partaking of a father and daughter chat, he was reticent (don't get me wrong, I loved him like crazy). My mother even said that I was a carbon copy of my father, I thought so too. It's just that my Daddy was what I call "Old School." When it comes to the facts of life (that was my Mom's job) and bringing home the bacon, egg, and bread (was my Dad's). And the entire neigborhood knew it, too.

On the other hand, my mother wasn't afraid to open up, ask or answer any questions. Mommy always added more than her two cents, every chance she could and sprinkled some true love over whatever she said. Our mother and daughter chats were priceless, and when we finished, I'd hug and kiss my Papi; because my Mami, said everything my Dad felt; but couldn't say. None of their parenting techniques were wrong; they were just different.

And that's what I love about both of them. One thing that always left me speechless was that my parents were in sync with each other was this.

> Proverbs 13:20 (NCV)
> Spend time with the wise, and you will become wise,
> but the friends of fools with suffering.

> "When someone loves you, the way they talk about you
> is different. You feel safe and comfortable."
> ~ Jess C. Scott

Wow, my adolescent years, I'm going to be sincere, I didn't always agree with everything my folks said, but as I matured things started to sink in and finally, everything made sense. Without a doubt, you must have already grasped on how much I savored this program. However, what left a bad taste in my heart (literally speaking) was when the last episode said that the father (Da Lauria) died and the mother (Alley Mills) put on her brave face and began a new job. Just like in my home. My father was called first to the Lord's presence and my mother became the head of the house in every sense of the word.

Once again, I still let out a few tears from time to time, when I think about that last episode. You know why? On account of, that's what occurred in my life. My father passed away or in Christian terminology (he went home to be with the Lord) after a long and painful struggle with cancer. In my opinion, the best part about my Dad's passing was that his pain to came to an end.

I say this because a few days before his passing the Lord told me while I was praying that my husband should go straight to my parents home, after work.

God also told me to stay in my home with our four infant sons; because my father wanted to give his life to Jesus Christ and his last wish was that my husband prays over him, too.

Life can be funny and painful at the same time. God told me that my father's wish was that my husband present to my Papi the plan of salvation, then he would leave in peace. Thank You, Lord, for that.

As soon as my Dominican Danish of a husband arrived at my folks home, the first words that came out of my Papi's mouth were this "I was waiting for you all day," and it's time for me to get right with God. My Dad continued the conversation in a soft pit voice.

The exchange of words went like this.

My father, son your the only that can guide me into the Lord's presence.

My husband said it would an honor.

It feels like yesterday, but it isn't; however, the best part about all of this is that one day my Papi (my father) and I will be reunited in Heaven (Yes Lord).

Even though a vast majority of my friends were watching television shows that were only centered around: sex with benefits, drugs and alcohol usage, while, I was teased for watching a comedy/drama called "The Wonder Years."

Don't misinterpret what I'm about to say; but, I can honestly raise my hands and praise the Lord (in a loud and proud way) because every time I bumped into one of my childhood friends, I do feel sorry for them. The reason being, during our teenage years, all they wanted to do is quibble and make reckless decisions.

I feel sorry for them every time their names pop into my mind, and now I truly understand the essence of this Bible verse.

> Proverbs 14:12 (NVC)
> Some people think they are doing right, but in the end,
> it leads to death.

God is interested in developing your character. At times He lets you proceed, but He will never let you go too far without the discipline to bring you back. In your relationship with God, He may allow you the right to make a wrong decision, but that's only so the next time you make the right one. Then the Spirit of God causes you to recognize that is not God's will. He guides you back to the right path.

Now and then, life can be so amusing when you're a teenager; but in the midst of my pre-adult years, I've learned so many valuable lessons without even knowing it. For instance, I sincerely understand the essence of this.

> Galatians 6:7-8 (NASB)
> 7. Do not be deceived, God is not mocked; for whatever
>   a man sows, this he will also reap.
> 8. For the one who sows to his flesh will from the flesh
>   reap corruption, but the one who sows to the Spirit will
>   from the Spirit reap eternal life.

If you happen to be a young lady or man reading this book, don't give in to peer pressure or social norms and ask (pray) to the Lord to provide you with the courage to be true to yourself and to embrace the healthy advice that your parents share with you, too.

The bible is full of a variety of healthy tips that talk to every age group and here's something helpful for all of those teens in need.

> Romans 12:2 (HCSB)
> Do not be conformed to this age, but be transformed
> by the renewing of your mind, so that you may discern
> what the good, pleasing, and perfect will of God are.

Thank You, Jehovah (God) because the Holy Spirit is verifying that someone is receiving healing. I feel it in my spirit, and I give God "all" the Glory, too.

Returning to the analogy about The Wonder Years. This show re-confirmed that all those long and severe talks between my parents and I weren't a waste of time. On the contrary, they were the heartfelt, life lessons and non judgemental. Our four outspoken sons (they're respect-ful when it comes to voicing their opinions), like to ask us questions, share they're opinions and thank us for being so honest (thank You, God, for that).

Moms, Dads, and other guardians don't ever give up on your daugh-ter or son; because you're not in agreement with the way they conduct themselves. But instead, bend your knees and seek the Lord's direction.

The Wonder Years touched a lot of topics, but what upset me a bit is the manner in which today's shows want to sugarcoat or ignore what our young people are going through now.

As a wife, mother and Pastor it only motivates me to pray more, keep the lines of communication open between my husband and our four sons more. Because I firmly believe that the foundation of any in-fant or teen's success story starts at home.

> 1 Timothy 5:8 (ESV)
> But if anyone does not provide for his relatives, and
> especially for members of his household, he has denied
> the faith and is worse than an unbeliever.

When I look at 1 Timothy 5:8 what stands out in my mind is that a lot of people in and outside of the Body of Christ think that this verse only refers to providing financial wise to their offsprings. But they're not correct, I take this verse to the level that we as parents should also have to truly listen to what our daughters and sons are sharing with us.

Because, I'm the type of mother that's continually reminding our four sons that their conduct says more than a thousand words.

All in all, this is the genesis of so many reasons why I love being a writer. Once again, thank You, God.

> We never know the love of a parent until we become parents ourselves.
>
> ~ Henry Ward Beecher

Jesus Christ indeed taught me how to appreciate life more, laugh, cry and enjoy my loving family (in every sense of the word) and not be afraid to set goals and eventually reach them, too. I'm so blessed to serve a Gracious God; on account of He has opened my eyes, mind, and heart to so many unique approaches on how to obtain mindful lessons during difficult times.

That's why I write these words, not with my pen, but with my heart; because when I was alone, bewildered and in severe pain, You (Lord) came to my rescued and consoled me like no one else. You're the antidote to everything in my life, and that's what I'm going to share with the world, everything I write. #Hallelujah.

Until the next time dear readers,

I bid you all a fond adieu....